# MIRACLE MOMENTS IN
# BASEBALL

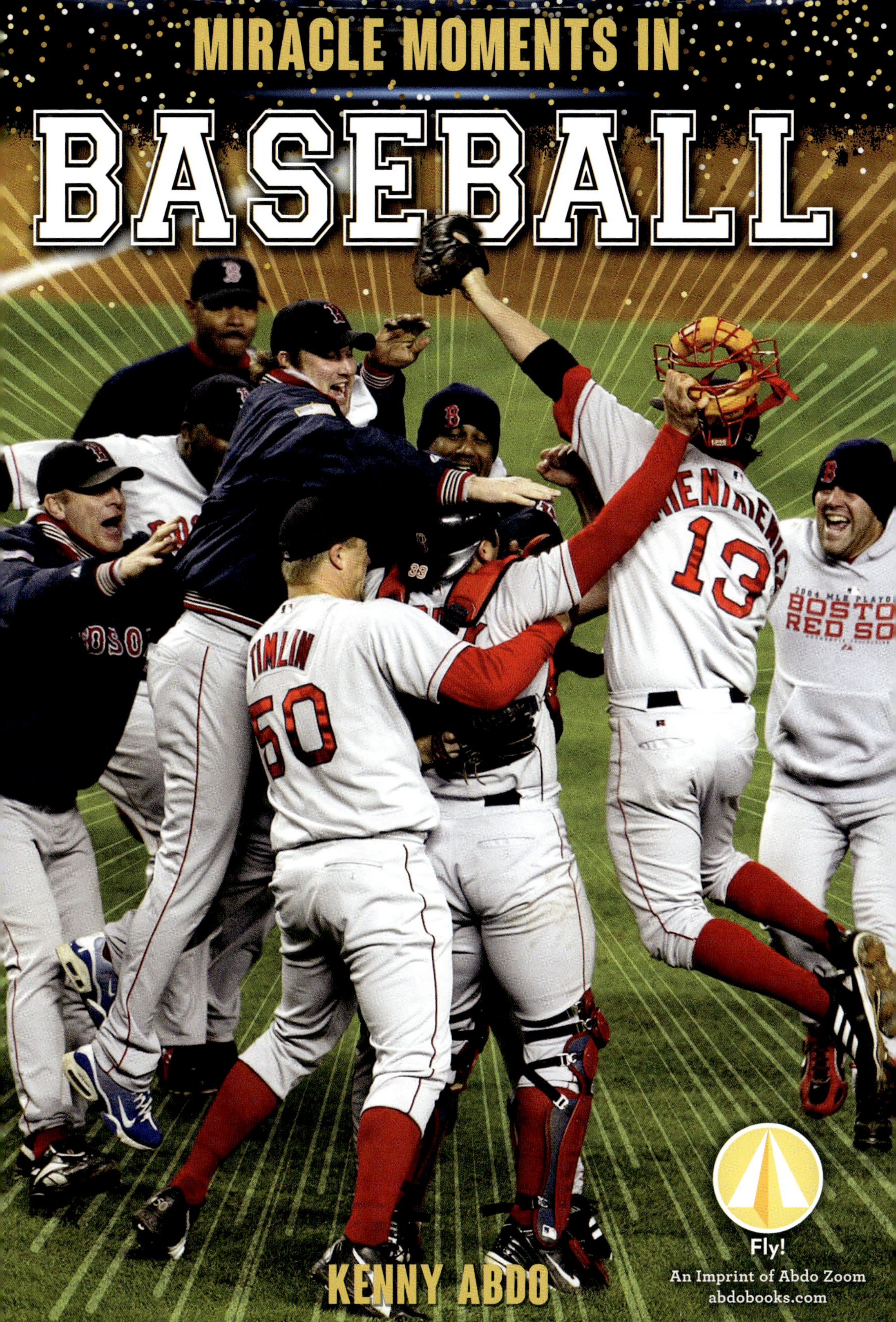

KENNY ABDO

**abdobooks.com**

Published by Abdo Zoom, a division of ABDO, P.O. Box 398166, Minneapolis, Minnesota 55439. Copyright © 2022 by Abdo Consulting Group, Inc. International copyrights reserved in all countries. No part of this book may be reproduced in any form without written permission from the publisher. Fly!™ is a trademark and logo of Abdo Zoom.

Printed in the United States of America, North Mankato, Minnesota.
052021
092021

Photo Credits: AP Images, Everett Collection, Icon Sportswire, iStock, Newscom, Shutterstock
Production Contributors: Kenny Abdo, Jennie Forsberg, Grace Hansen
Design Contributors: Dorothy Toth, Neil Klinepier

**Library of Congress Control Number: 2020919508**

**Publisher's Cataloging-in-Publication Data**

Names: Abdo, Kenny, author.
Title: Miracle moments in baseball / by Kenny Abdo
Description: Minneapolis, Minnesota : Abdo Zoom, 2022 | Series: Miracles in sports |
    Includes online resources and index.
Identifiers: ISBN 9781098223182 (lib. bdg.) | ISBN 9781098223885 (ebook) |
    ISBN 9781098224233 (Read-to-Me ebook)
Subjects: LCSH: Baseball -- History.--Juvenile literature. | Baseball--Records-
    Juvenile literature. | Sports--History--Juvenile literature. | Miracles--Juvenile
    literature. | Curiosities and wonders--Juvenile literature.
Classification: DDC 796.357--dc23

# TABLE OF CONENTS

# BASEBALL

Rightly called America's "national **pastime**," baseball is one of the most popular sports in the world!

Bat and ball games have been around for centuries. It wasn't until 1839 that the word "baseball" was invented along with its rules and field design.





7

From called shots to breaking century-long curses, fans have witnessed a handful of miracles on the baseball diamond.

# DO YOU BELIEVE?

In 1932, Babe Ruth pointed with his arm toward the center-field bleachers at Wrigley Field. He slammed the ball in that exact direction into a crowd of 50,000 crazed fans. The Yankees went on to win 7 to 5.

The Giants needed a miracle to secure the **pennant** against the Dodgers in 1951. In the bottom of the ninth of a tied game, Bobby Thomson hit a home run **clinching** the win. It was called the "Shot Heard 'Round the World."

Mickey Mantle pulled a muscle in his left forearm during a 1961 game against the Detroit Tigers. At risk of being **benched**, he said his arm was fine. Holding the bat with just his right fist, he launched the ball for his 49th and 50th home run of the **season** that game. The Yankees won a three game **sweep**.

The Atlanta Braves led the 1991 **World Series** against the Minnesota Twins. Kirby Puckett was 3-for-18 hits the entire series. In the bottom of the 11th inning of a grueling tied game 6, Puckett finally hit a homer. The Twins won the World Series the next night!

The Red Sox won the 2004 **World Series** for the first time since 1918 to break the **Curse of the Bambino**. The Sox did it again, sweeping the Rockies in 2007. They **clinched** more victories in 2013 and 2018, assuring fans that the first win wasn't just a fluke.

# LEGACY

Baseball miracles have captured the imagination of audiences in every medium. From books to movies like *61**, *The Sandlot*, and *Field of Dreams*. *Fever Pitch* crews had to quickly rewrite the end of the movie because of the Red Sox's unexpected 2004 victory.

For almost 200 years, baseball miracles
have made an already beloved sport
even more wonderous to its fans.

# GLOSSARY

**benched** – taking a player out of the game for a certain amount of time.

**clinch** – to confirm a win.

**Curse of the Bambino** – an 80-year period of not winning the World Series for the Boston Red Sox after they traded Babe "Bambino" Ruth in 1918.

**pastime** – an activity people participate in for their enjoyment.

**pennant** – a flag representing a sports championship.

**season** – the portion of the year where certain games are played.

**sweep** – winning a series of games without any losses.

**World Series** – a yearly series of games, where the team who wins a best-of-seven playoff is determined the champions of the year.

# ONLINE RESOURCES

**Booklinks**
**NONFICTION NETWORK**
**FREE!** ONLINE NONFICTION RESOURCES

To learn more about miracle moments in baseball, please visit abdobooklinks.com or scan this QR code. These links are routinely monitored and updated to provide the most current information available.

# INDEX